Seeders

Lori Dittmer

CREATIVE EDUCATION

CREATIVE PAPERBACKS

seedlings

Published by Creative Education and Creative Paperbacks
P.O. Box 227, Mankato, Minnesota 56002
Creative Education and Creative Paperbacks
are imprints of The Creative Company
www.thecreativecompany.us

Design by Ellen Huber; production by Joe Kahnke
Art direction by Rita Marshall
Printed in the United States of America

Photographs by Alamy (Ed Buziak, clynt Garnham Agriculture,
Matt Limb OBE, SergBob), Getty Images (Andrew Sacks),
iStockphoto (aarows, arrogant, kamski), Minden Pictures (Nigel
Cattlin), Shutterstock (Africa Studio, Vereshchagin Dmitry,
Fotokostic, Anatoliy Kosolapov, oticki, Olga Popova, Straight 8
Photography, Valentin Valkov, ZoranOrcik)

Library of Congress Cataloging-in-Publication Data
Names: Dittmer, Lori, author.
Title: Seeders / Lori Dittmer.
Series: Seedlings.
Includes bibliographical references and index.
Summary: A kindergarten-level introduction to seeders,
covering their purpose, parts, role in farming, and such
defining features as their hoppers.
Identifiers: ISBN 978-1-60818-911-3 (hardcover) / ISBN 978-1-
62832-527-0 (pbk) / ISBN 978-1-56660-963-0 (eBook)
This title has been submitted for CIP processing under LCCN
2017940115.

CCSS: RI.K.1, 2, 3, 4, 5, 6, 7;
RI.1.1, 2, 3, 4, 5, 6, 7; RF.K.1, 3; RF.1.1

First Edition HC 9 8 7 6 5 4 3 2 1
First Edition PBK 9 8 7 6 5 4 3 2 1

TABLE OF CONTENTS

Hello, seeders!

Seeders are farm machines. Tractors pull them across fields.

Farmers use seeders for sowing. Seeders make small furrows. Then they drop seeds and fertilizer.

Hoppers are bins that hold seeds. Air pushes the seeds through tubes. This keeps the seeder from dropping too many seeds.

Some seeders toss seeds all over a field. Others plant in rows. They can plant many rows at once. Some drill each seed into the ground.

Wheat seeds are small.
Other seeds are larger.

Farmers use the seeder that works best for their crop.

Seeders drop seeds in fields. They cover the seeds with dirt.

Now plants can grow.

Goodbye, seeders!

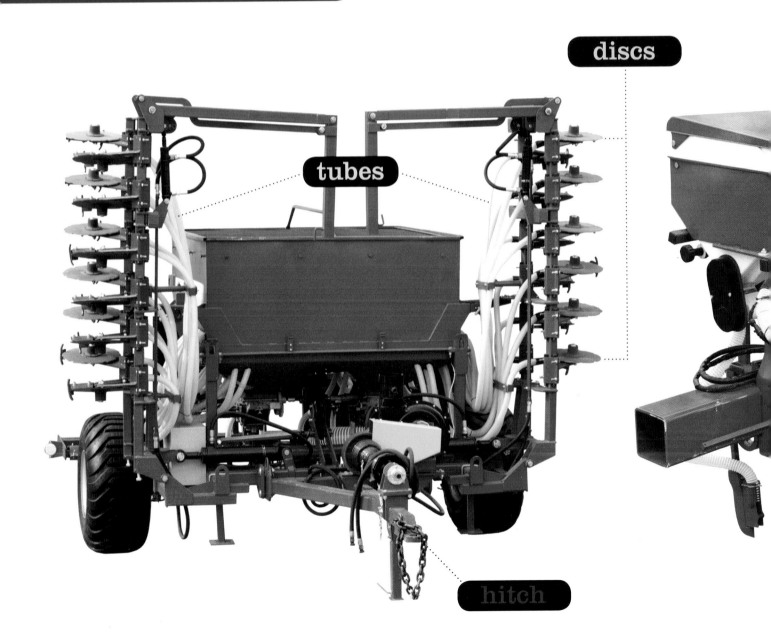

discs

tubes

hitch

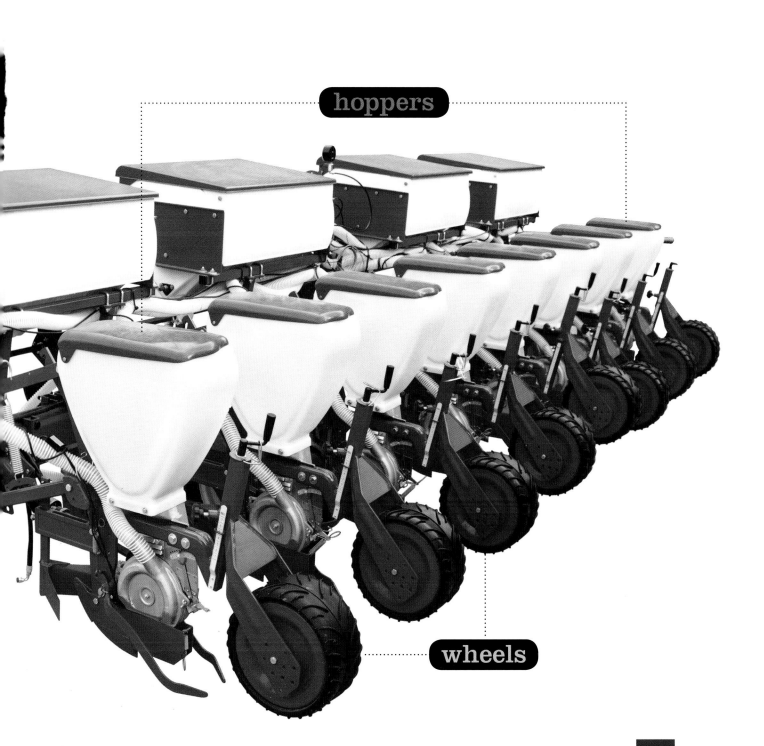

hoppers

wheels

crop: a plant that is grown for people or animals to eat and use

fertilizer: a substance that is added to dirt to help plants grow

furrows: straight, narrow rows for planting seeds

sowing: planting seeds

Read More

Dufek, Holly. *Planters and Cultivators.*
Austin, Tex.: Octane Press, 2016.

West, David. *Farm Machinery.*
Mankato, Minn.: Smart Apple Media, 2015.

Websites

Kids Farm
http://www.kidsfarm.com/wheredo.htm
Learn about farm equipment and animals from a farm
in Colorado.

**Tractors for Kids – Learn Farm Vehicles
and Equipment with Blippi**
https://www.youtube.com/watch?v=ZyEnVLPhjUc
Watch a video to learn more about farm machines.

Index